Architectural Monographs No 18

FRANK LLOYD WRIGHT

THOMAS A HEINZ

A.D. ACADEMY EDITIONS / ST. MARTIN'S PRESS

Architectural Monographs No 18
Editorial Offices
42 Leinster Gardens London W2 3AN

ISSN 0141-2191

Editorial and Design Team
Andreas Papadakis (Publisher)
Andrea Bettella (Senior Designer)
Vivian Constantinopoulos (House Editor)
Annamarie Uhr (Designer)
Lisa Kosky (Designer)

All colour photographs are by the author

Subscriptions
Mira Joka

Cover: Taliesin West, Scottsdale, Arizona, 1938; *P2*: Barnsdall House, Los Angeles, California, 1923.

First published in Great Britain in 1992 by
ACADEMY EDITIONS
An imprint of The Academy Group Ltd
42 Leinster Gardens London W2 3AN

ISBN 1 85490 105 2 (HB)
ISBN 1 85490 110 9 (PB)

Published in the United States of America in 1992 by
ST MARTIN'S PRESS
175 Fifth Avenue, New York, NY 10010

ISBN 0-312-07243-0 (HB)
ISBN 0-312-07149-3 (PB)

Printed and bound in Singapore

FRANK LLOYD WRIGHT

THOMAS A HEINZ

CONTENTS

ABOVE: **Framing**, Willits House, Highland Park, Illinois, looking east. The living room is on the left with the entry door at the centre. The stone foundation is easily seen.
BELOW: **Walls**, Taliesin, Spring Green, Wisconsin, looking east. Some of the best stone work Wright ever used is contrasted with the smooth stucco of the living room.

EVIDENCE OF INTELLIGENCE

Thomas A Heinz

Frank Lloyd Wright's buildings are not just differently designed, they are differently constructed. Wright had to invent or re-invent many items and systems to bring about his new art. Every design, every hidden detail, is evidence of Wright's unique intelligence.

Many aspects of Wright's work remain largely untouched. Wright was a masterful engineer as seen in the Unity Temple's structural system and again in the Prairie House attic trusses. Even if all of his drawings were published, the engineering side would still be largely missing; so few drawings concerning the structural details remained in the architect's office. Most of the structural drawings were sent out to the engineer or contractor during construction as original drawings instead of blueprint copies. During the rebuilding of the living room of the Little House at the Metropolitan Museum of Art in New York, drawings concerning the structural beams were misleading and never touched upon the clerestory window support rods.

Some areas worth investigation are touched upon in this book including structural systems, interior aerodynamics, construction material suitability and maintenance, lighting and colour. Investigations would require considerable on-site work. Since more and more of Frank Lloyd Wright's buildings are in the public sector, in so many parts of the country, these might be tapped as a point of beginning.

NEVER SAY NEVER

Wright cannot be pinned down to hard-and-fast rules and practices. In every building he experimented with something, always testing the conventions of architecture. The terms 'always' and 'never' just do not apply, not even when Wright himself says so. For instance, he said he never used the 'guillotine' window after the Winslow House of 1892. But the kitchen and meeting rooms at the south end of Unity Temple (1906) have many double-hung windows. He claimed he banished basements from the Prairie House, but he used basements in the Willits, Cheney, Little and Martin Houses. Defining the Prairie House as a strip of windows under low-pitched, widely overhung roofs points up the exception that is the Mrs Thomas Gale House of 1909.

Other architects who designed in the Wrightian mode often were more consistent than the one who originated the style, and, in fact, some of their creations are more apt to appear as the quintessential Prairie House than are many of Wright's, with his little quirks and exceptions.

THE SETTINGS

1 Site: Clients seldom ask an architect's advice when they purchase land and the architect is limited to choosing the location of the building on it. Whatever the site, Wright planned the structure to work with the land. The Willits House site is flat, with many towering American elm trees – hardly a prairie. The lawn was to be grass with no foundation planting. While the early houses were quite horizontal in orientation, they also were fairly tall, such as the William Martin and Fricke Houses of Oak Park.

On Wright buildings it is sometimes difficult to tell where the building begins and the land ends. The Darwin Martin House of Buffalo is the best example of the site integration of the early period, with its low brick walls that extend from the building and set off the planters. Taliesin is 'of the hill'. The Hardy House of Racine is part of the bluff above Lake Michigan, as the unbuilt Morris House is designed to be out of the cliff. The Lake Tahoe buildings seem, as do the Los Angeles concrete block houses, to grow out of their sites and add to their surroundings. Fallingwater adds to its site but, unlike the others, there is nothing to see from the house but foliage. Even the stream and waterfall are invisible except from the edge of the balcony. Wingspread spreads over the flat site and appears to initiate the ravine that starts at the east side of the house, while by contrast, Aline Barnsdall's Hollyhock House perches on the hill.

2 Landscaping: Most Wright buildings look better without the typical foundation planting. In the early days of Wright's career, Walter Burley Griffin, an 1899 University of Illinois graduate, and Jens Jensen, a Chicago landscape designer, prepared planting plans based on the Prairie tradition as first outlined by Wilhelm Miller.

Most of the early houses were designed without much planting. The later Usonian buildings often included vegetable gardens along with a lot of defining foliage. The Zimmerman House landscaping (New Hampshire) reportedly was designed by Wright.

FROM THE GROUND UP

3 Footings and Foundations: How much does it take to support a one- or two-storey building? Instead of four-foot-deep poured concrete foundations over one-by two-foot footings, Wright's Usonian houses often used a simple but effective combination of a trench filled with large gravel. Most water would drain off, and any residual moisture would expand into the air voids between the individual stones as it froze. Two well-known buildings in which he used this method are the first Jacobs House and the Unitarian Church, both in Madison, Wisconsin.

The Willits House and Wright's Oak Park House are both supported by stone foundations and both have full basements. The Heurtley House, in contrast, incorporates the poured concrete foundation into the exposed curb at the building's base to support the brickwork above. Square concrete blocks in the basement seem to penetrate the concrete floor slab and are apparently the tops of some piles.

4 Framing: The wall construction of the majority of the early buildings were fairly conventional two-by-four studs or masonry with sawn lath over furring or studs. But the Jacobs House has 'sandwich' walls. The plywood core screwed to tongue-and-groove siding is thin and non-loadbearing, but the wood adds considerably to the insulating and acoustical qualities of the wall.

5 Walls: The Willits House stucco lath has expanded metal – a new material at the time – and the house was featured in the manufacturer's advertising. A smooth sand-finish stucco with the colour mixed in was used as the final of three coats. The plaster was often 'burned' by overtrowelling while the plaster was drying. This technique gave a certain swirled texture that had lots of pores of various sizes. This texture looked darker in sunlight and lighter when it was overcast because of the shadows in the pores from the sun – the appearance is different every day. The Dana and Tomek Houses are the last to have these original walls.

The Ennis House and the other California block houses all are constructed using a textile block system of wire fabric and concrete block. The Usonian Automatic ideas, from the 1950s, are an extension of this 1920's practice using the same construction principles.

The difference was that the clients themselves should manufacture the blocks, which would significantly lengthen the construction process but drop the cost to a fraction.

Wingspread, Johnson's Wax Administration Building, and the Wiley House are brick inside and out, but all have cavities that contain insulation. The Wiley House, like the earlier Heurtley House, uses alternating colours of face brick. On the Heurtley House, the lighter narrow-striped colour is set off from the darker red brick to create a tapestry effect similar to that often used and advocated by Louis Sullivan.

The Winslow House plaster frieze, according to written descriptions, was originally about the same colour as the brick. The same was true of the Husser and Heller Houses. The Dana House has yielded some evidence that the original frieze and brick colours were closely matched. The friezes themselves are made of common wall plaster and gypsum plaster, with horse-hair as binder and reinforcement.

Wright didn't use sawn cedar shingles very often, but when he did, he usually introduced a board beneath some of the rows to give the appearance of wood board-and-batten siding. In the Romeo and Juliet Windmill, he used this shingle technique, and in 1894 he put a board beneath every third row of shingles on the Peter Goan House of LaGrange.

6 Windows: Once Wright latched onto the casement window, he rarely used any other style, but he did continue to experiment, however, with things like Luxfer Prisms and, in the Johnson Wax Building, clear Pyrex tubing. Since nearly all windows were custom-made, he could choose the most flattering proportions for each building, whether the sash was designed to hold his art glass or for simple ventilation.

The two most famous examples of Wright's use of double-hung windows are in the Winslow House and Unity Temple. Probably because of the poor ventilating qualities and the mechanical problems that come up with the counterweights or springs, Wright virtually abandoned this style of window very early.

In 1897, Wright became architectural adviser and consultant to the newly incorporated Luxfer Prism Company. His two facade designs are well known but fairly impractical uses of the prism lights and the only place it seems that Wright actually used them was in the south basement window in his Oak Park House. Bruce Pfeiffer of the Frank Lloyd Wright Memorial Foundation has said that some drawings of the Johnson Wax Building indicate that Wright considered using prisms in the late 1930s even though the company went out of business in 1924.

ABOVE: **Roofs**, Taliesin, looking east. A very early Henry Fruerman photo contrasts with the gently rolling hills of the Taliesin valley. The sawn cedar shingles give a very crisp appearance to the randomness of the stonework. BELOW: **Walls**, Willits House. While technically not a wall, it does all of the things a wall would do except block all views through it. This view is from the library above the entry up into the bedroom hallway.

ABOVE: **Living room**, Taliesin. This photo is from about 1928. The ceiling is like that at the Barnsdall House in Los Angeles. It seems unusual that there is so little Wright-designed furniture (see page 14 for a different view of the same room). BELOW: **Dining room**, Willits House. The built-in cabinets were a simple extension of the rest of the woodwork for the house. It appears that Wright never designed a sideboard that was not a built-in unit.

7 Entry and Front Doors: The front doors of most Wright houses are solid panels, either flush or decoratively divided, with an occasional peephole or small window. The majority of his early house doors, however, are the style-and-rail type. Wright's first commission, the Winslow House, incorporates a stunning example of Sullivan ornamentation in its stylised seed pod of an oak leaf motif. In the Willits House, the door slab has two vertical panels, in a variant of style-and-rail. The door of the Harry Adams House of Oak Park diverges significantly, with its long, thin slits filled with random squares of beautiful iridescent, translucent glass. This pattern is not a carryover of the window pattern, but is more like the pattern used in the strips of squares that run through the clerestory windows of the Coonley playhouse. In Wingspread, as with many of the Usonian houses, the door is similar to the casement windows, with a glass panel in a style-and-rail frame. The alternative for many Usonians was a simple flush panel slab.

The Winslow House has a centrally placed front door on the street front, with a concrete walkway leading directly up to it. This was Wright's first commission, and about the last time he used such a direct approach. The Willits House entry is fairly typical of Wright's early period. Before visitors enter the building, they are covered by a roof, enclosed by walls on three sides, and are virtually inside without yet going through a door. The Cheney entry is even longer: the visitor begins at the front corner (either corner), walks along a concrete and brick walk, ascends several stairs, walks further along and strolls past brick piers, turns left and climbs more stairs, turns left and up more stairs, turns right up some more stairs, walks under the roof and finally is facing the front door, which is at the centre of the south wall. Other entries offer a circuit not quite so long but equally interesting and varied.

8 Roofs and Roof Pitches: The roofs of most Prairie Houses are pitched four in twelve. Wright used standard four-ply felts of asphalt on his nearly flat roofs, but he covered the dead-flat roofs with coal tar pitch. While the roof of the Willits House and several other of the early houses use wood shingles, Wright was fond of red clay tile which he used on Wingspread and the Dana, Coonley and Zimmerman houses. The more exotic roofing materials include his use of metalwork in the Marin County Building and the two-inch square blue ceramic tiles of the Annunciation Greek Orthodox Church in Milwaukee.

9 Structural: Wright employed ingenious structural solutions to building problems; unfortunately, little of it shows up in his drawings. The Willits House has two two-foot trusses in the attic, where they are seldom used. At the inside corner of the second floor front balconies, rods connect the attic trusses to the north/south ceiling beams in the living room. In the outside walls steel columns rise from the foundation to support the ends of the attic trusses and ceiling beams of the living room. Trusses are also found in the attics of the Cheney and Heurtley Houses. These are much deeper units – as much as seven feet deep.

The Coonley House has no attic above the living room, and it utilises a very different system of support for the roof and ceiling. A stiff steel frame begins in the second window mullion from the corner in the side walls and incorporates a moment connection that attaches to a beam running through the ceiling plane and joins at the peak with other beams that spring from the outside edges of the chimney.

10 Cantilevers: The basic rule of thumb for engineers using cantilevers is two-thirds supported and one-third cantilevered. However, when one examines the carport canopy at the entrance to the Carroll Alsop House in Oskaloosa, the reverse is true: it is a two-thirds cantilever. Wright was a genius, but one doubts that he reversed the laws of physics. Two things make the Alsop cantilever possible. First, there are two stiffeners inside the edge of the canopy; second there are rods that pierce the fireplace and extend into the chimney footing to hold the one-third end.

The thick-and-thin aspect of some of Wright's cantilevers is easily seen in the overhang of the front of the roof of the Hickox House of Kankakee. It tapers to a knife edge, but the trim hides the thickening of the plane, which significantly stiffens it.

The reconstruction of the living room of the Little House shows another example of cantilever. The trellises that extend over the bay windows are balanced over those windows with the ceiling inside. In fact, the 2 x wood members start at the trim at the window heads, extend over the bay windows, and then cantilever out in space.

11 Trusses: Beside the trusses in the attics of the Willits, Cheney and Heurtley Houses, an interesting truss situation is hidden in the walls of the porches in the rear of the Bach House in Chicago. A beam runs across the top of the hefty support, extending to the outside of the porch. The truss buried in the wall supports the cantilever past the supports and connects back to the main section of the house.

12 Rods: Rods hold up the living-room ceiling of the Willits House, and a series of rods keeps the cantilever of the roof/ceiling/trellis in place in the Little House. Rods are contained in the mullions of the casement windows of the clerestories. The rods extend from deep steel beams in the attic space through the clerestory window mullions and, for the reconstruction, end in small metal bars that are buried in the 2x that cantilever over the bay windows.

The second Jacobs House, the solar hemicycle, employs rods to support the second floor much as the Little House bay ceiling is supported. Rods that connect to bars in both the roof and floor structure keep the nuts from pulling through the wood. The forty-five-degree wood siding that makes up the partitions on the second level also acts as a diaphragm and keeps the floor structure from swaying, as it is not attached to the front window-wall.

13 Plumbing: It is well known that Wright used the earliest wall-hung toilets in the Larkin Building. The method relates to the desk chairs that he hung from the sides of desks – both the toilet rooms and the offices became easier to clean.

14 Electrical: Wright's Oak Park house appears to have been prepared for electricity, and certainly the 1895 remodelling of his dining room was the earliest indirect lighting that has been documented. The idea of bare-bulb track lighting and wiring troughs was employed in the living room of the first Jacobs House of the 1930s. Wright apparently did not invent any special switching or low-voltage uses. His wiring and switching was typical of then-current conventions.

15 Mechanical Heating and Cooling: The Willits house radiators were in metal ducts that ran horizontally below the living- and dining-room floors. Continuous cast grilles ran along each side of both rooms, allowing heat to rise into them without obstructing a view or requiring radiators that needed to be integrated and covered. Fresh-air intakes were integrated into the exterior base trim, and the whole mechanism apparently worked. A similar system of below-floor radiation is used on the south side of the Robie House living rooms, while radiators are hidden behind wood grilles along the north wall.

In Usonian houses, Wright frequently installed heating pipes below the concrete slabs. This radiant heat keeps one's feet warm, even though the air temperature may be low, making the room feel comfortable.

Buffalo's Larkin Building was Wright's first attempt to temper forced air not only with heat but also with cooling and humidity. Carrier, who worked in the same town, is usually credited with the earliest development of air conditioning; Wright is rarely mentioned. Jack Quinnan's recent book, *Frank Lloyd Wright's Larkin Building*, has the latest and best information about the building. Some of Wright's later buildings, such as the Hanna and Friedman Houses, use forced-air heating systems. The rest get along quite well with radiant heat.

16 Interior Aerodynamics: Not many people seem to know much about this important subject, but Wright appears to have dealt with it masterfully. After many smoke experiments in the living room of the Heurtley House, it appears that the geometry of the house causes a definite pattern of air circulation, with the covers on the radiators contributing to this effect. The heat is forced to rise upward rather than radiate outward. Rising air creates a vacuum inside the cover, so cooler air is pulled in from the floor, which results in air currents.

Two buildings on which the porches have not been converted to rooms or screened in – the Pettit Chapel and the Gridley House – also indicate a basic airfoil in the design of the pitched roofs of the porches and walls. A minor vacuum seems to be created by any breeze and is further enhanced as the air is pinched between the top of the wall and the edge of the overhang. Insects do not linger in this air flow, making for a pleasant outside space. In the 1901 Foster House, one can create a breeze inside the house with various combinations of open and closed windows. In the Tomek House, one must be judicious about how many windows are opened or the wind created may knock over the flower vases on the tables and send magazines careering onto the floor.

The Usonian houses also seem to create their own breezes if certain combinations of doors and clerestory windows are opened, as demonstrated at the Pope-Leighy House. Wright seemed to understand and design for rising hot air and sinking cold air, although he never discussed it in print. More needs to be explored in this particular area.

INSIDE

17 Living Rooms: Wright's living rooms are complex in their spatial make-up. Two of the best examples are the Willits and William Martin Houses. The earlier Willits House has an area at the east end that includes a low-ceilinged entry, a fireplace seating area and an entryway into the dining room. And that covers only about one-fifth of the room. The rest is a single large space, with

ABOVE: **Bedroom**, Taliesin. In contrast with the earlier bedrooms of Taliesin, this view is a good example of the openness caused by the sloped ceilings. BELOW: **Bedroom**, Wright House, Oak Park, Illinois. The beds were designed in the mid-teens and are quite similar to those of the Sherman Booth House. This is Wright's own bedroom.

ABOVE: **Living room**, Coonley House, Riverside, Illinois. This room has the same dimensions as that of the Heurtley House but appears much larger because of the spatial extensions along the mural wall. This is one of the first rooms to have oak ceiling trim that is discontinuous. The rug on the floor is described in the **Colour** section. BELOW: **Chimneys and Fireplaces**, Taliesin, living room. Early living room much like the one for the Pew House of Madison built in the late thirties.

ceiling beams and built-in casework along two walls. The design creates two spaces in one room.

The William Martin House living room is arranged in a pinwheel design. The centre of the wheel is a little built-in seat at right angles to the fireplace. Opposite is a bench seat under the window overlooking the front yard and next to the French doors leading to the front stoop. The double wood ceiling trim echoes the pattern, with one strip following the wall and the other defining the square.

The Robie House living room originally had a bench at the fireplace. The rear of the bench contained a bookcase topped by spindles that did not reach the low ceiling. This bench defined a sub-space within the room. In the living room at Taliesin, a fireplace bench without spindles accomplished the same purpose; it extended into the room and had an attached table.

The central living space at Wingspread also contains several spaces in one room. It takes the pinwheel idea of the William Martin House and adds a third dimension to it by extending it through three levels. These levels include three desk areas, a dining space, three attached benches as living areas, and a mezzanine leading to the north bedroom wing.

18 Dining Rooms: Nearly all of Wright's dining rooms feature built-in casework rather than leaving space for owner-purchased furniture. The Willits House dining room, for instance, has a set of drawers and cabinets with glass cases on top. As is seen in the often-published views of the dining room at the Willits House, the chairs create a sub-space within the room itself. In the Dana and Boynton Houses, Wright added breakfast areas, spaces that are a part of the dining rooms but closer to the outside windows with lower ceilings and their own sets of furniture.

19 Kitchens: J Kibben Ingalls of River Forest was involved in refrigeration – something quite new at the turn of the century – and his Wright-designed house had an early refrigerator. The majority of the early kitchens were designed to be used by hired cooks and servants. The Usonian houses, such as the Hagan House near Fallingwater, offered kitchens of adequate size, but the locations often did not allow for a window to the outside. Instead, skylights were the norm. Knowing that heat, cooking gasses and odours rise, Wright often made the kitchen ceiling the highest in the house.

20 Bedrooms: Bedrooms were called 'chambers' in the early schemes. Their size was proportionate to the size of the building and included closet space that was deemed adequate at that time. The Usonian era brought about a rethinking and a reallocation of space within the dwelling. These bedrooms were of minimal size, with limited functions. Often a desk would be built in and space allotted for a single bed and clothing storage. What would have been more generous bedroom floor space was shifted into the larger living-room spaces, where several family members could participate in activities.

21 Bathrooms: When personal hygiene practices changed, so did bathrooms; as what was once a weekly event became a daily routine, more facilities were added. But along with the reallocation of space, bathrooms shrank. In some of the Usonian houses the showers are so small that one has to exit the stall to raise one's hands and elbows above the head.

22 Chimneys and Fireplaces: Wright's chimneys were not mere masses of brick but well thought-out, multifunctional constructions. One such unit is the Cheney House fireplace, which incorporates a skylight that lights the inside of the attic and extends the light into the rear bedroom hall; and he might put a fireplace anywhere, not only in the interior. In the Mrs Thomas Gale House in Oak Park, the fireplace is in the east wall of the living room. Wingspread has five flues in one central chimney. The fountains in the Dana and Bogk Houses are placed as if they were alternatives to chimneys, even though both houses also had fireplaces.

Fireplaces were very important parts of the interior design of Wright's buildings. The majority of the firebox openings are square or rectangular, with a few arches. The early unit for the drafting room of Wright's studio was arched, as is the firebox in the sitting room at the Darwin Martin House. The most classic rectangular design is that of the Coonley House living room. The upper part is set out slightly and rests on a horizontal limestone mantle. The limestone cubes at the floor set off the edges of the firebox.

The Hanna House living room fireplace reflects the hexagonal theme of the house. The Pew House of Madison has a stone chimney and hearth similar in many ways to the early scheme for the living room fireplace at Taliesin. Usonian fireplaces, however, were much more varied in design and configuration.

23 Lighting: Because electrical lighting was so new, most of the Prairie Houses use it sparingly – one might think of it as stage lighting. The general illumination level is high enough so that one has enough light to avoid bumping into the furniture, and Wright adds what today is called task lighting for reading, dining or playing the piano. The Robie House introduces different lighting options in its sunlight/moonlight (direct/indirect) lighting of the main living rooms.

24 Colour: The Coonley House has yielded unique information about Wright's use and coordination of colours. During a recent remodelling, the removal of wall coverings exposed the original wall surfaces. The murals adjacent to the living room fireplace were gone and only the raw plaster remained. The ceilings still are all a sheepskin colour, as they were when the house was built. The plaster panels on the walls of the living room are green and the dining room red. Samples of the original rug yarn colours mirror the plaster colours. In addition, the golden tan rug border matched the original wood colour of the cabinet doors and drawers, which is still visible on the inside. The lime green of the art glass windows also appeared as a large field in the carpet. A part of the carpet pattern is a deep blue that one can only assume was from the bedroom wing since it did not appear in the west – living/dining – side of the house.

Seeing these colours come to life, one can get a sense of the colour descriptions that Wright outlined in the *Architectural Review* of 1900 that Wilburt Hasbrouck reprinted several years ago. The description of the Winslow House indicated that the roof, frieze and the brick were all nearly the same colour, a fact that is borne out in early photos of the house. This contrasts with the beautiful chocolate-brown frieze and white stone trim that we see today. The Heller House brick and frieze also are in the same colour family. The *Architectural Review* wrote:

> Interior is finished in simple materials, rough plaster and soft wood stained. Exterior of hand made brick and undressed wood. The whole washed with stain. Colour schemes soft brown outside developing to polychromatic arrangement of rich low tones. Inside chairs and tables covered with leather bands. Floors with dark brown linoleum. – *Wright's Studio*
> Exterior walls faced with vitrified buff Roman brick, between second- and third-storey sill course grey brick alternate with buff. Attic storey treated in high relief. Soffits panelled with perforated apron dropped inside outer band. Trimmings grey stone. Roof covering of flat red tiles. All horizontal joints white, vertical joints colour of brick. Interior walls of rough sand finish, trimmed in quartered and waxed white oak. Plaster saturated with pure colour. Floors' finish and furniture of one wood

and colour throughout, lighting fixtures in main rooms wooden standards with globes worked in brass and opalescent glass. Interior colour scheme bronze and dull green. – *Heller House*
> Exterior of bright golden Roman brick, frieze in relief, pink tile roof, buff Bedford trimmings. Approach of stone and cement with mosaic inlay. Mosaic platform before entrance door worked in polychromatic pattern with 1/4 inch tesserae. Interior in polished white oak. Colour scheme olive green cream and tan. – *Winslow House*
> Exterior walls faced with dry-yellow Roman bricks. Horizontal joints wide and raked out to emphasise horizontal grain, vertical joints stopped flush with mortar the colour of the bricks. Stone trimmings, terracotta capitals, frieze in stucco relief, soffits plain in plaster, roof covering of light red flat tiles without modelled trimmings. Hips and ridges clean. Interior walls of lower entrance and principal rooms lined with slender Roman bricks, light tan in colour carrying gold insertion, and inlaid bands of olive oak, plaster dead gold. – *Husser House*

Green seems to have been Wright's favourite colour in the Prairie period – as most exteriors have some green in them. The Usonian era focused more on reds and browns, as in the brick he used so frequently.

In the 1950s Wright collaborated with the Martin-Senour Paint Company and issued a colour palette that seemed to cover most of what he used throughout his career. It is at least a point of beginning for anyone looking for a direction exploring Wright's use of colour.

25 Furniture: The finest of all of the Prairie-era furniture that has come to light thus far is from the Dana House. The line, proportion and attention to detail is unsurpassed. The double tapering of the back leg of the tall-backed dining chair, coupled with the depth of the upper style and restraint of the seat trim, combine to make the most elegant and delicate of all Wright's tall-backed dining chairs. There is no other building with as much existing original furniture. It has recently been refinished and is now on display as a part of the tour of the house.

The Usonian period saw a basic change in the furniture, much of which was constructed of plywood instead of solid stock. Often, it was made by carpenters on the site; in some cases, the owners themselves built their furniture from Wright's plans, as did Paul Hanna.

Many of the sizes and heights are the same from the early period to the later designs. The tables are mostly twenty-eight inches high, compared to the industry standard of thirty inches, and the chairs are proportionally lower than standard.

Of the many ensembles Wright designed and constructed, one of the most unusual was the design and arrangement of the living room furniture in Kaufmann's Fallingwater. The three heights of the little egg-crated tables, the stools, hassocks and coffee tables were arranged in two groupings: one at each of the two built-in seats at the east and south sides of the living room. The plans show a layered, interdigitated grouping that gave the arrangement a dynamic appearance, subtly but significantly different from its current plan.

26 Stained Glass: Nowhere is Wright's mastery of the nature of materials more apparent than in his glass art. The Dana House contains the best examples. Nearly every plane has a different but related abstract design. The subtle colour changes and choices of the iridescent cathedral glass make these designs come alive. The bold, graphic use of thick and thin metal came adds so much to the design that it seems amazing it has not been replicated, even after almost ninety years. This house also contains some of Wright's first three-dimensional art glass designs in the table lamps and other light fixtures.

27 Ceramics: Wright's designs extend to nearly all materials. The fountain and the statue, 'Flower in the Crannied Wall', at the entrance of the Dana House are great examples. Wright also designed the terracotta work on the west facade of the Bogk House in Milwaukee.

His designs in concrete include the statuary and panels for Midway Gardens, German Warehouse and the bridge in Glencoe at the Booth House. The patterns expressed in the concrete blocks of the early California houses follow this same theme – to integrate the design and the material. These designs could not, indeed, should not, be transferred to other materials, such as wood or fabric.

28 Graphic Design and Murals: While much of the work of any architect involves a certain amount of graphic art, Wright's designs for his buildings and other items extend far beyond the norm. The earliest work he was involved in was the murals in the bedroom and playroom of his Oak Park House. Orlando Giannini was the executing artist, but the bold use of arcs and stripes were likely Wright's.

The next most important work was the abstract murals for Midway Gardens. These panels were lost when the building was demolished. We may never know about the colour scheme, but the patterns themselves are documented in the Wendigen books. The next murals were for the dining room of the Imperial Hotel in Tokyo. Much larger and more complex, they appear a bit overwhelming and perhaps were not as successful as those of Midway Gardens.

29 Fabrics and Rugs: An interior would not be complete without fabrics and rugs, and one would scarcely expect Wright to leave the design to others' choice. The Coonley rug was discussed in the Colour section. The original drawings and yarns of the Robie House rugs were consulted to create reproductions that were recently installed in the house, which is open for daily tours. Carpets were also designed for some of the Decatur houses but only the drawings now exist. The Milwaukee Art Center has on display the original rug from the Bogk house. The same patterns were used for the rug that is now in the house, but Mrs Wright appears to have chosen a new colour scheme after Wright died. Among other changes, the deep red field was changed to an orange. The Barnsdall House has carpets of Wright's original design, but the coloration is by the late Lloyd Wright, Frank Lloyd Wright's architect son who oversaw the construction and restoration. A very small fragment of the original rug from the Imperial Hotel is a part of the Domino's Pizza Collection and is worth seeing. The only existing original rug that remains *in situ* is in the David Wright House in Phoenix.

CHARNLEY HOUSE, 1891

ABOVE, BELOW AND FACING PAGE: Done while with Sullivan; now the headquarters of SOM Foundation which is sometimes open to the public.

McARTHUR HOUSE, 1892

ABOVE: Dining room corner bay. Already Wright is opening up the corners of the rooms. The structure is taken out of the corner to let more light in.

ABOVE: Dining room, McArthur House. The built-in cabinet on the left was added in a 1901 remodelling but the overall detailing and woodwork is original.

WINSLOW HOUSE, 1892

FACING PAGE ABOVE: Entry interior. The warm oak wood tones parallel the orange brick on the exterior. Surprisingly, there is little metalwork in the house of an executive of an architectural metal foundry. The frieze murals are later additions. FACING PAGE BELOW: South wall of dining room. The oak columns and carved capitals differentiate the main dining area from that of the breakfast bay. The Dana and Blossom Houses had similar layouts. OVERLEAF: West front. First commission on his own. An expression of 'where does the building end and the land begin?'

MOORE HOUSE, 1895

ABOVE: Exterior. This house was rebuilt in 1923.

ABOVE AND OVERLEAF: Exterior, Moore House.

EMMOND HOUSE, 1892

OPPOSITE PAGE ABOVE: A brick base with clapboard above is an unusual mix of materials not seen again until the 1906 Beach House of Oak Park.

BAGLEY HOUSE, 1894

OPPOSITE PAGE BELOW: Exterior. The library on the north or left is nearly identical in plan to Wright's office built in 1897.

HELLER HOUSE, 1896

ABOVE: South entry. A beautifully detailed limestone entry with offset columns is more typical of the era than of Wright's design progress to this point.

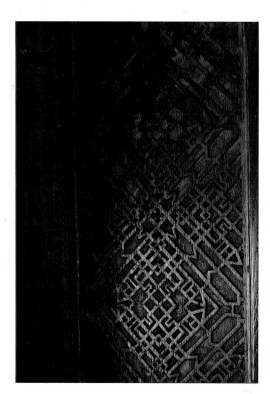

ABOVE LEFT: Living room fretwork, Heller House. Much of this fretwork had fallen into disrepair when this photograph was taken, but what is there is original. ABOVE RIGHT: Stair balusters. Wright's work is associated with close set square spindles. Here is an example of tapered and round units.

ROMEO & JULIET WINDMILL, 1896

FACING PAGE: East side. Originally sheathed in sawn cedar shingles like many of HH Richardson's work, this design is a fine example of engineering. The vertical wood members are bolted to steel straps embedded into the concrete and stone foundation taking the stresses directly.

WILLIAMS HOUSE, 1897

ABOVE: East front. Across the back yard, east of the earlier
Winslow House, is this early design.

ABOVE LEFT AND RIGHT: Dormers, Williams House. A rare
example of Wright's design progression, showing the original
dormer with the bay spanning the arch followed in 1901 by an
alteration that added a steep roof mirroring the main roof and a
cantilevered brow above new fenestration. FACING PAGE: Front
entry door. Local lore has it that Williams, Winslow, Wright and
Waller gathered these boulders from the Des Plaines River
running just west of Waller's House that once stood across the
street from Winslow's.

SMITH HOUSE, 1897

ABOVE: West front. A mix of wood trim and shingles make for an unusual material mix. The wood trim making the corners is almost lost. This house has the same flared base as the Davenport House.

FURBECK HOUSE, 1897

ABOVE: Living room.

LINCOLN CENTER, 1899

FACING PAGE: South front. Many proposals were submitted before this was accepted, which was done in association with Dwight Perkins. Very similar in colouring to the Larkin Building.

BRADLEY HOUSE, 1900

OVERLEAF: Living room, east end. The original furniture in locations similar to those first published. The furniture is now all sold and out of the building.

THOMAS HOUSE, 1901

ABOVE: Living room. A very unusual arrangement with little space in front of the fireplace and a large soffit adjacent gives no clue to use or furniture arrangement.

ABOVE: Entry, Thomas House. After threading through a circuitous entry route one is rewarded by this effusion of glass in a type of mystery box: all panels look the same but only two are actually doors. OPPOSITE PAGE BELOW: Dining Room. The first gabled-ceiling dining room is overwhelmed by a large breakfront that has details in smaller scale than those on the exterior.

HENDERSON HOUSE, 1901

OPPOSITE PAGE ABOVE: West facade. With a nearly identical plan to the Hickox House of Kankakee and the Cheney House of Oak Park, the elevations are hipped and much more enclosed and solemn.

WILLITS HOUSE, 1902

ABOVE: West front. The Willits family lived in this house well into the 1950s.

ABOVE LEFT: West front, Dutch doors, Willits House. ABOVE RIGHT: Living room cabinet. With the back removed, the composite steel form is exposed. This column extends up into the attic and supports the end of a truss holding a rod which helps to support the living room ceiling.

FRICKE HOUSE, 1902

OPPOSITE PAGE ABOVE AND BELOW: West facade. This powerful design with few windows is one of the tallest Wright houses in Oak Park, Illinois.

DANA HOUSE, 1902

ABOVE: Dining room frieze. This delicate frieze may have been partially lost in earlier cleanings. Each day's light shows it differently.

ABOVE: Ballroom. This is the most deceiving room of the house. There are arches on the north and south sides of the main space that hold up the roof so that the windows on those facades can be as light and tall as possible – much like the reverse of a flying buttress. OPPOSITE PAGE ABOVE: South and east fronts. The frieze was removed for safety reasons just before the building was sold to the state of Illinois. The original frieze was about the same colour as the brick. OPPOSITE PAGE BELOW: The ballroom, south front. This pavilion holds the ballroom on the upper level and the library on the lower. OVERLEAF: Living room. A large but uninspiring room has a very thick, heavy and disproportionate ceiling trim.

ABOVE: Sculpture, 'Flower in the Crannied Wall', Dana House. This sculpture greets you as you enter the south front door – a sort of a take-off of knowing where the sculpture ends and the body begins. Modelled by Richard Bock and produced by William Gates at the Teco Potteries of terracota. A similar unit was installed in the gardens at Taliesin but is now largely destroyed.

ABOVE: Entry fireplace. One of five fireplaces in the house, this arch reflects the butterfly arches of the entry door. The assembly of glass, furniture and andirons are in a nice material harmony.

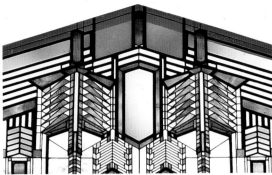
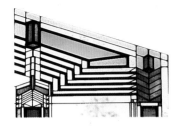

ABOVE TOP ROW: Front windows. Unfortunately, all the windows in the house have now been covered over with tinted storm windows. ABOVE LEFT: Entry light. This simple form contains a complex pattern as the simple design of the dining room light is in a complex form. ABOVE RIGHT: Hanging light. Now popularly known as 'the butterfly light', it contains several optical illusions.

ABOVE: South front. A very direct entry for such a complex house is a deceiving introduction.

LITTLE HOUSE, 1903

ABOVE: Master bedroom. A spacious room which is nearly as big as the living room below. The beds are original to the house.

ABOVE: Master bedroom ceiling light.

BARTON HOUSE, 1903

OPPOSITE PAGE ABOVE: Dining room. OPPOSITE PAGE BELOW: Living room. This was the first house Wright designed for Darwin Martin, with whom he continued to work for many years.

HEURTLEY HOUSE, 1903

OVERLEAF: West front. This is one building that changes character with the everchanging light. The broad overhangs, the canted walls at the base, and the textured banding of the bricks all contribute to the advantages it takes of the light. PAGES 50-51: Living room, interior. The low overhang of the roof eave accentuates the height of the interior ridge.

WILLIAM A MARTIN HOUSE, 1902

ABOVE AND BELOW: Living room. A small intimate room for the size of the house, it feels larger because of the openness into the dining room beyond.

DARWIN D MARTIN HOUSE, 1904

ABOVE: Living room. The wood ceiling trim is newly installed and adds immeasurably to the sense of space. These rooms are another example of a three-part space like the Cheney, Hickox, Elmhurst, Barton, South Bend Houses. They all feel much larger than they actually measure.

ABOVE LEFT: Entry stairs, Martin House. A two storey space in an otherwise horizontal house, the doorway originally led out a long corridor to the conservatory. ABOVE RIGHT: Lawn ornament. Richard Block modelled four different designs based on the four seasons. These plus a full sized unit are now down at a small college outside St Louis, Missouri. OVERLEAF: South front. One of the five great houses of Wright's Prairie period, this house has had a very hard life having been abandoned for fifteen years and is now underfunded by the current public ownership.

WESCOTT HOUSE, 1904

ABOVE: South front. One of the few definitive Prairie houses by Wright. The symmetry, strip windows, wide eaves and stucco give a quiet look. The east or left elevation is in contrast quite tall.

CHENEY HOUSE, 1904

ABOVE: Living room.

GLASNER HOUSE, 1905

FACING PAGE ABOVE AND BELOW: Living room. An overly sensitive architect introduced these rods, not trusting Wright's engineering.

TOMEK HOUSE, 1906

ABOVE: South front. The first try of a design that would develop into the Robie House a few years later. OPPOSITE PAGE ABOVE AND BELOW: Living room. With its triple ceiling lights, it is quite similar to the Boynton House.

ABOVE LEFT: Living dining hall, Tomek House. The passageway that connects the living and dining rooms on the south side of the entrance is as constricted as that of the Robie House. ABOVE RIGHT: Exterior detail, Tomek House.

HUNT HOUSE, 1906

OVERLEAF: Living room interior. The first house built on the 'Fireproof House for $5000 Design' first published in the 1901 Ladies' Home Journal was constructed out of wood frame and stucco.

UNITY TEMPLE, 1906
ABOVE: Skylight.

ABOVE: Entry doors. OPPOSITE PAGE ABOVE: East exterior. In contrast to the church across Lake Street which was built later, Unity Temple not only looks more modern but also larger when it is actually much smaller. OPPOSITE PAGE BELOW: Temple room interior. By designing two tiers above the main floor, Wright was able to compress more people into a smaller volume than most assembly spaces and yet one does not feel cramped. OVERLEAF: West exterior. One of the finest abstract compositions of Wright's career, the obvious but distanced entry is at the centre with the Temple room on the left and the social hall on the right.

ABOVE: *Interior lighting detail, Unity Temple. The hanging corner lights of the temple room tie the space together vertically but also give it depth by providing close and far focusing points.*

ABOVE: *Detail of skylight, Unity Temple.* OPPOSITE PAGE: *Stair window. One of eight tall strip windows that define the corner piers on the exterior, lighting the otherwise dark tampole stairs.* PREVIOUS PAGE: *Entrance.*

HEATH HOUSE, 1907

OVERLEAF: *Living room. Missing the hanging glass lights it still retains the stickley craftsman furniture. The carpet, Scandinavian coffee table and dog are recent additions.*

STOCKMAN HOUSE, 1908

ABOVE: North elevation.

COONLEY HOUSE, 1908

ABOVE: South elevation. This facade has been altered three times, twice by Wright. The copper clad timbers add considerably to its three dimensional effects.

GILMORE HOUSE, 1908

FACING PAGE ABOVE: Front. FACING PAGE BELOW: Living room.

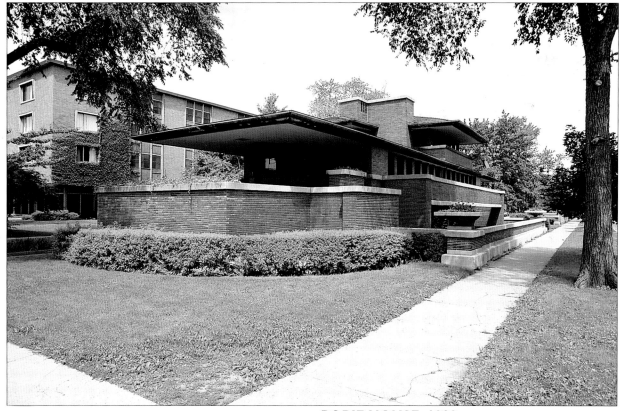

ROBIE HOUSE, 1909

*ABOVE: South front. The classic Wright Prairie House and its
wide overhanging eaves with their crisp edges sitting in the city.*

*ABOVE: East living room, Robie House. The bench seat to the
left of the fireplace is now missing which has lessened the severe
symmetry. The cantilevered couch in the foreground is a recent
production.*

DAVIDSON HOUSE, 1908

*OPPOSITE PAGE ABOVE AND BELOW: Living room. The largest
and most open of all the two-storey living rooms. This house is
the only one without a balcony.*

IRVING HOUSE, 1909

ABOVE: South facade. Symmetrical and strongly horizontal.

BALCH HOUSE, 1911

ABOVE: East facade. Nearly across the street from Ernest Hemingway's house, the disproportionate design appears to have little of Wright's influence and was perhaps designed while he was away in Europe.

LITTLE SUMMER HOUSE, 1913

FACING PAGE ABOVE: North facade. Now demolished and partly reconstructed at the Metropolitan Museum of Art in New York and the Allentown (Pennsylvania) Art Museum, this building takes to the contours of the land. FACING PAGE BELOW: Looking east to the dining room. This complex building expressed each space on the exterior.

IMPERIAL HOTEL, 1916

ABOVE: Exterior. These photos are of the reconstruction in Meiji Mura Park near Nagoya. The scale is deceivingly small as is that of the Larkin and Johnson's Wax buildings.

ABOVE: Entrance, Imperial Hotel. FACING PAGE ABOVE AND BELOW: Exterior and interior.

TALIESIN HOUSE, 1911-1959

PREVIOUS PAGE: Lake elevation. One of the most beautiful places on earth, the building landscape and the intimate scale are in perfect harmony.

MUNKWITZ APARTMENTS, 1916

ABOVE: West facade. Now destroyed by a street widening project, these were to be low-cost prefabricated units. They were not far from the Richards Brothers' development south on 27th street at Burnham.

RICHARDS' TYPE PREFAB HOUSE, 1916

ABOVE: Exterior.

BOGK HOUSE, 1916

FACING PAGE ABOVE: Exterior. All trim is made of terracotta in a similar style to that of Midway Gardens.

HAYASHI HOUSE, 1917

FACING PAGE BELOW: Exterior. This is really the most 'Wrightian' detail of this perplexing house.

FREEMAN HOUSE, 1923

ABOVE: Living room. Wright's original furnishings were replaced by designs by Schindler which transformed the feeling of the space.

ABOVE: Living room, Freeman House.

MILLARD HOUSE, 1922

OPPOSITE PAGE: South front. At the bottom of the small inset, just two blocks above the Rose Bowl, sits this textured textile block house, the first of its kind. It still survives the earthquakes.

STORRER HOUSE, 1923

ABOVE LEFT: South front detail. This amalgamation of several different concrete block designs blends well for a pleasant overall effect. ABOVE RIGHT: Top room. The living room has an excellent view of the Los Angeles valley to the south. In concept it is very similar to the Willits House living room of twenty years earlier.

ABOVE: Bedroom, Storrer House. All four bedrooms are identical and are separated by bathrooms on both floors. The glass frame on the left slides over the pierced block to close the 'window'. FACING PAGE ABOVE: Exterior.

BARNSDALL HOUSE, 1923

FACING PAGE BELOW: Exterior. This house was designed as early as 1919. OVERLEAF: West living room. The original furniture has been reconstructed from photos and drawings.

ENNIS HOUSE, 1924

ABOVE: Living room. One of the most complex spaces since the Dana House, this space is unchanged since the original construction.

ABOVE: Hallway, Ennis House. A straight hallway that runs the entire length of this two-bedroom house is probably the longest of Wright's entire career.

JONES HOUSE, 1929

FACING PAGE ABOVE AND BELOW: Living room. The concrete block system used here is similar to that used in the Los Angeles houses except that here the voids are used for forced air heating and lighting.

JOHNSON HOUSE, 'WINGSPREAD', 1937

ABOVE: Interior, second floor.

ABOVE: Aerial view. PREVIOUS PAGE: Exterior from the east.

TALIESIN WEST, 1938

ABOVE: Theatre interior. Used for movies and for formal Saturday night dinners, the white Italian lights are usually associated with Christmas but here they give a glow to the whole room. Wright often uses low wattage bulbs in multiples for a soft effect somewhat like the light at dawn or dusk.

ABOVE: Exterior. OVERLEAF: South drafting room facade. One of the most striking settings for a remarkable building. The gathering storm clouds reinforce the jagged geometry.

ABOVE: Exterior, Pope House. The house was dismantled and moved to the Woodlawn Plantation at Mount Vernon because of impending road construction that was never completed.

STURGESS HOUSE, 1939

ABOVE: Living room. The room lighting is much like the 1923 Freeman House with its cave and field effects.

LEWIS HOUSE, 1940

OVERLEAF: Living room. Notice how the line of lights and wood pierces the glass transom to the study.

JACOBS HOUSE, 1943

ABOVE LEFT: Exterior detail. The stone at the ends of the curved window walls actually serve to buttress the forces of the facade.

ABOVE AND TOP RIGHT: Second floor. The steel rods hanging from the roof support the floor without having either columns or extensions to the front window wall. OPPOSITE PAGE ABOVE AND BELOW: Living room. The living/dining room is one long curved space, undifferentiated except for the fireplace.

SMITH HOUSE, 1946

ABOVE: South facade. One of many variations of the first Jacobs House of 1936, this house has one of the most tranquil settings at the edge of a small pond frequented by Great Blue herons, Canada geese and Mallard ducks, and is situated just down the road from Saarinen's Cranbrook school.

ABOVE: Wood screen, Smith House. The wood screen pattern was later used for doors in the dining room.

MILLER HOUSE, 1946

FACING PAGE ABOVE: Facade. FACING PAGE BELOW: Side. The standard red brick is substituted here by beautiful stone.

UNITARIAN CHURCH, 1947

OVERLEAF: West front. One of the most copied designs of Wright's non-residential output, this church was built by Marshall Erdman (of the Wright pre-fab), on a trench foundation filled with gravel.

ADELMAN HOUSE, 1948

ABOVE: Living room. The warm wood offsets the coldness of the concrete block.

ABOVE LEFT: Bedroom. Original drawing on the wall, lighting above closets. ABOVE RIGHT: Hallway. While small in width, the clerestory relieves the claustrophobic feeling. OPPOSITE PAGE ABOVE AND BELOW: Yard facade. An extremely long house, emphasised by the alternating colours of the concrete block and the strip of the bedroom windows.

MOSSBERG HOUSE, 1948

ABOVE: Bedroom. Very much like the top floor of Fallingwater with the small bed area and adjacent windows opening onto a terrace.

ABOVE: Dining area. The brick floor contrasts with the white fluffy carpet of the living room with the bench that seats many. FACING PAGE ABOVE: South and east facade. Apprentice Jack Howe was not only involved in the design but also in supervising the construction of this house for a printing executive. FACING PAGE BELOW: Living room. A large area with many small spaces within the same room.

ALSOP HOUSE, 1948

ABOVE: East facade.

MORRIS GIFT SHOP, 1948

ABOVE: South facade. A masterful use of brick, the beautiful iron spot brick field is offset by the alternating voids on the left.

ZIMMERMAN HOUSE, 1950

ABOVE: The complexity of the wood detailing in the built-in shelving and the cornice above not only saves having to purchase separate cabinets but also fully integrates all the materials in the house.

ABOVE: Living room. Quite similar to many of the later houses with the entry and closet leading past the fireplace into the main space with the dining room to the south. FACING PAGE ABOVE: North entry. The small-scaled entry is inviting with its boulder. This house is now in the custody of the Currier Gallery, an institution that was designated to take over the house by the original owners. FACING PAGE BELOW: Guest bedroom. A small but very pleasant room on the south overlooking the backyard, it is directly off the kitchen and dining area.

HARPER HOUSE, 1950

ABOVE: South elevation. The flat site seems dull in contrast to the dramatic bluff view of Lake Michigan to the west.

KEYES HOUSE, 1950

ABOVE: North entry facade. The realisation of the workers' cooperative housing for Detroit is a second example of bermed designs by Wright.

WRIGHT HOUSE, 1950

OPPOSITE PAGE ABOVE: An interesting mix of geometrics come together at the end of the house. The jagged edge of the roof makes the line seem severe. OPPOSITE PAGE BELOW: East bedroom wing. Being constructed in the desert, it is unusual that this house lifts off the ground rather than going into it adding to its ability to gain heat.

ADELMAN HOUSE, 1951

ABOVE: Entry. A concrete block pavilion house, it backs up to the Arizona Biltmore property and is next to the Boomer House.

WRIGHT HOUSE, 1953

ABOVE: Living room. A lozenge-shaped house with lozenge shaped furniture designed for his youngest son, a prominent Washington attorney.

WALKER HOUSE, 1950

OPPOSITE PAGE ABOVE AND BELOW: Exterior. The stonework has a similar feel to the Unitarian Church of Madison. This house is one of more than twenty stone houses of the Usonian period.

HAGAN HOUSE, 1954

ABOVE: Kitchen/Entry. Partitions without doors effect the same privacy and distinction of space as those with doors only with more surprises.

ABOVE: Dining room. The table slab was made by George Nakashima, a famous woodworker. FACING PAGE ABOVE: Entry. In a valley not far to the north is Fallingwater. The house surrounds an auto paddock and looks out over the beautiful Appalachian valleys. FACING PAGE BELOW: Living room fireplace. This photograph was taken before the devastating fire and remodelling, and shows the beautiful stonework.

LOVNESS HOUSE, 1954

ABOVE: Living room. This house was completely constructed by the Lovnesses as was the nearby cottage and all the furnishings.

ABOVE: Dining area. An oversized fireplace dominates the room that has little freestanding furniture. The chairs were originally designed for the Barnsdall House and are now part of the Domino's collection in Ann Arbor, Michigan. FACING PAGE: Interior. Beautifully executed, the south facing cottage uses the stone floor to store solar radiation to keep the dwelling warmer at night. OVERLEAF ABOVE: Bedroom. The closet doors are from the Little House in Northhome. OVERLEAF BELOW: South bedroom. The hot water radiant heat keeps the bedroom warm. The cast iron wicket is from Sullivan's Owatonna Bank.

PAPPAS HOUSE, 1955

ABOVE: South entry facade. A Usonian Automatic that was actually built in accordance with Wright's ideals, by the owner casting the block and assembling them into a house.

KUNDERT MEDICAL CLINIC, 1955

ABOVE: Exterior. A local attraction attested to by the sign at the curb, has cut wood screens and obscure glass.

BETH SHOLOM SYNAGOGUE, 1957

ABOVE: A striking example of the assimilation of many cultures.

ABOVE: Interior. Translucent panels replace the stained glass of usual religious buildings. FACING PAGE: Ridge detail. These finials soften the otherwise sharp edges of this prism.

KALIL HOUSE, 1957
ABOVE: *South facade. These Usonian Automatic houses were more varied than most of Wright's later designs.*

FASBENDER CLINIC, 1957
ABOVE: *Exterior.*

MARIN COUNTY BUILDING, 1957
FACING PAGE: *This dome contains the county library and appears to be the 'hinge' for two wings. OVERLEAF: The largest Wright design ever constructed was largely built after his death in 1959. The rhythm of the arches is similar to that of musical notes.*

FRIEDMAN HOUSE, 1959

ABOVE: Entry hall. Like the William Martin house of 1902, the entry allows one to observe the living room without entering the room.

ABOVE: Entry hall. FACING PAGE ABOVE: Wood fret grille. While all of the wood grilles are similar, they vary within a range much like snowflakes. FACING PAGE BELOW: Living room. The plaster ceiling is unusual in later Wright houses. The built-in bench seating adjacent to the fireplace is another control Wright designs into his living rooms.

LIST OF PROJECTS

James Charnley House,
1365 North Astor Street, Chicago, Illinois, 1891

Warren McArthur House,
4862 South Kenwood, Chicago, Illinois, 1892

Herman Winslow House,
Edgewood Place, River Forest, Illinois, 1892

Robert G Emmond House,
109 South 8th Avenue, LaGrange, Illinois, 1892

Frederick Bagley House,
121 County Line Road, Hinsdale, Illinois, 1894

Nathan G Moore House,
Forest Avenue, Oak Park, Illinois, 1895, rebuilt 1923

Isadore Heller House,
5132 South Woodlawn Avenue, Chicago, Illinois, 1896

Romeo and Juliet Windmill,
Tani-deri Hill at Taliesin, Spring Green, Wisconsin, 1896

Chauncey Williams House,
Edgewood Place, River Forest, Illinois, 1897

George W Smith House,
Home Avenue, Oak Park, Illinois, 1897

George Furbeck House,
223 North Euclid Avenue, Oak Park, Illinois, 1897

Lincoln Center,
Chicago, Illinois, 1899

R Bradley House,
Kankakee, Illinois, 1900

Henderson House,
Elmhurst, Illinois, 1901

Frank Thomas House,
210 Forest Avenue, Oak Park, Illinois, 1901

Fricke House,
540 North Fair Oaks, Oak Park, Illinois, 1902

Ward W Willits House,
Sheridan Road, Highland Park, Illinois, 1902

Susan Lawrence Dana House,
Lawrence Avenue, at 4th Street, Springfield, Illinois, 1902

George Barton House,
118 Summit Avenue, Buffalo, New York, 1903

Francis Little House,
Moss Avenue, Peoria, Illinois, 1903

Heurtley House,
Forest Avenue, Oak Park, Illinois, 1903

William A Martin House,
East Avenue, Oak Park, Illinois, 1902

Darwin D Martin House,
125 Jewett Parkway, Buffalo, New York, 1904

Edwin Cheney House,
520 East Avenue, Oak Park, Illinois, 1904

Burton J Wescott House,
1340 East High Street, Springfield, Ohio, 1904

William A Glasner House,
850 Sheridan Road, Glencoe, Illinois, 1905

Frederick F Tomek House,
150 Nuttal Road, Riverside, Illinois, 1906

Steven MB Hunt House,
345 South Seventh Street, LaGrange, Illinois, 1906

Unity Temple, Lake Street,
Oak Park, Illinois, 1906

WR Heath House,
76 Soldier Place, Buffalo, New York, 1907

EA Gilmore House,
120 Ely Place, Madison, Wisconsin, 1908

Dr GC Stockman House,
311 First Street, SE, Mason City, Iowa, 1908

Avery Coonley House,
Bloomingbank Road, Riverside, Illinois, 1908

Walter Davidson House,
57 Tillinghast Place, Buffalo, New York, 1908

Frederick C Robie House,
5757 South Woodlawn Avenue, Chicago, Illinois, 1909

EP Irving House,
2 Milliken Place, Decatur, Illinois, 1909

Oscar B Balch House,
611 North Kenilworth, Oak Park, Illinois, 1911

Francis Little Summer House,
Deephaven, Minnesota, 1913

Taliesin,
County C, Spring Green, Wisconsin, 1911-1959

Imperial Hotel Reconstruction,
Meiji Mura Park, Inuyama City, Japan, 1916

Arthur Munkwitz Apartments,
1102 North 27th Street, Milwaukee, Wisconsin, 1916

Richards Type Prefab House,
Wilmette, Illinois, 1916

Frederick C Bogk House,
2420 North Terrace Avenue, Milwaukee, Wisconsin, 1916

Aizaku B Hayashi House,
1-30 Komazawa 1-Chome, Setagaya-Ku, Tokyo, Japan, 1917

Yamamura House,
173 Yamate-Cho, Ashiya, Japan, 1918

C Jiyu Gakuen School,
31-34 Nishi Ikebukuro 2-Chome, Toshima-Ku, Tokyo, Japan, 1920

Alice Millard House, 'La Miniatura',
Pasadena, California, 1922

Sam Freeman House,
1962 Glencoe Way, Los Angeles, California, 1923

John Storrer House,
8161 Hollywood Boulevard, Los Angeles, California, 1923

Aline Barnsdall House, 'Hollyhock',
4800 Hollywood Boulevard, Los Angeles, California, 1923

Charles Ennis House,
Glendower, Los Angeles, California, 1924

Richard Lloyd Jones House,
3704 Birmingham Road, Tulsa, Oklahoma, 1929

Johnson House, 'Wingspread',
Four Mile Road, Racine, Wisconsin, 1937

Taliesin West,
Shea Boulevard, Scottsdale, Arizona, 1938

Lauren Pope House,
Woodlawn Plantation, Mount Vernon, Virginia, 1939

George D Sturgess House,
449 Skyeway Road, Brentwood, California, 1939

Lloyd Lewis House,
Little St Mary's Road, Libertyville, Illinois, 1940

Herbert Jacobs House,
3037 Old Saulk Road, Madison, Wisconsin, 1943

Melvin and Sarah Smith House,
5045 Pon Valley Road, Bloomfield Hills, Michigan, 1946

Dr Alvin L Miller House,
1107 Court Street, Charles City, Iowa, 1946

Unitarian Universalist Church,
900 University Bay Drive, Madison, Wisconsin, 1947

Albert Adelman House,
7111 North Barnett, Fox Point, Wisconsin, 1948

Herman T Mossberg House,
1404 Ridgedale Road, South Bend, Indiana, 1948

Caroll Alsop House,
1907 A Avenue East, Oskaloosa, Iowa, 1948

Morris Gift Shop,
140 Maiden Lane, San Francisco, California, 1948

Kenneth Laurent House,
Spring Brook Road, Rockford, Illinois, 1949

Isadore J Zimmerman House,
223 Heather Street, Manchester, New Hampshire, 1950

David Wright House,
5212 East Exeter Boulevard, Phoenix, Arizona, 1950

Ina M Harper House,
207 Sunnybank Road, St Joseph, Michigan, 1950

Thomas E Keyes House,
31 Skyline Drive, Rochester, Minnesota, 1950

Mrs Clinton Walker House,
Scenic Road, Carmel, California, 1950

Benjamin Adelman House,
5710 North 30th Street, Phoenix, Arizona, 1951

Robert Llewellyn Wright House,
7927 Deepwell Drive, Bethesda, Maryland, 1953

Isaac Newton Hagan House,
Ohiopyle Road, Chalk Hill, Pennsylvania, 1954

Don and Virginia Lovness House,
RR #3, Stillwater, Minnesota, 1954

TA Pappas House,
865 South Masonridge Road, St Louis, Missouri, 1955

Kundert Medical Clinic,
1106 Pacific Street, San Luis Obispo, California, 1955

Beth Sholom Synagogue,
Old York Road, Elkins Park, Pennsylvania, 1957

Kalil House, 117 Heather Street,
Manchester, New Hampshire, 1957

Fasbender Clinic,
Pine Street, Hastings, Minnesota, 1957

Marin County Building,
Redwood Highway 101, San Raphael, California, 1957

Allan Friedman House,
20 Thornapple, Bannockburn, Illinois, 1959

BIBLIOGRAPHY

Creese, Walter, *The Crowning of the American Landscape: Eight Great Spaces and Their Buildings*, Princeton University Press, Princeton, New Jersey 1985.

The Taliesin valley in Wisconsin is discussed as is the mountain slope that Taliesin West is on. A short history of the valley and maps make it well worth reading.

Gutheim, Frederick ed, *In the Cause of Architecture: Frank Lloyd Wright*, Architectural Record, New York 1975.

Not only a reprint of seventeen articles that appeared in *Architectural Record* between 1908 and 1952, but also several essays by scholars and former apprentices. Several of the 1928 articles discuss Wright's views on materials.

Hanna, Paul R and Jean S, *Frank Lloyd Wright's Hanna House: The Client's Report*, Second Edition, Southern Illinois University Press, Carbondale, Illinois 1981, 1987.

Paul Hanna was not only a Wright client but also the Social Studies editor of World Book Encyclopedia for thirty-five years. The Hannas acted as contractors through the several phases of construction. The text is well documented and references the Hanna archive now at Stanford.

Heinz, Thomas A, *Architectural Design*, 1/2 1980, p68-71, 'Frank Lloyd Wright: Dana House 1903'.

This article contains a few colour interior photos taken before the reworking of the house in the late 1980s.

Heinz, Thomas A, *Fine Homebuilding*, June/July 1981 No 3, p20-27, 'Frank Lloyd Wright's Jacobs II House'.

A through discussion, with illustrations, of the many innovative structural and construction techniques used in a never repeated Wright design.

Heinz, Thomas A, *Old House Journal*, September/October 1989, p35-38, 'Use & Repair of Zinc Cames in Art-Glass Windows'.

Focused on Wright examples, this short article discusses construction techniques and graphic consequences of zinc came.

Jacobs, Herbert, *Building with Frank Lloyd Wright: An Illustrated Memoir*, Chronicle Books, San Francisco 1978.

A great piece of writing by a former newspaperman and his wife about two significant Wright designs. There are many construction photos with accompanying information and insights into the buildings and the people who got them built.

Kaufmann, Jr, Edgar J, *Fallingwater: A Frank Lloyd Wright Country House*, Abbeyville Press, New York 1986.

It took a long time to finally get the whole story on this remarkable structure but here it is in a most beautiful presentation. While it dispels many of the myths about the house, it brings to light even more remarkable true stories.

Lynch, Mark David, *Frank Lloyd Wright Newsletter*, three articles: Volume 2, Number 2, p12-17, 'Ward Winfield Willits: A Client of Frank Lloyd Wright'; Volume 2, Number 3, p1-5, 'The Ward Willits House by Frank Lloyd Wright'; and Volume 3, Number 1, p7-11, 'Design Origins of the Ward Willits House'.

Three fine articles that explore many unknown pieces of information, and several rare photographs, including a few of the building under construction.

Miller, Wilhelm, *The Prairie Spirit in Landscape Gardening*, Urbana: University of Illinois, 1915, Circular 184.

Showing examples of Wright and other Chicago architects that make up a group using native plants to enhance their buildings, it is hoped that someone will reprint it.

Pearson, (Anderson), Gay, *Frank Lloyd Wright Newsletter*, Volume 4, Number 1, First Quarter 1981, p1-5, 'The Muirhead House: An Interview with Robert and Betty Muirhead'.

An excellent essay about the only farmhouse Wright designed. The article includes photographs taken during different phases of construction showing the trench foundation and the placement of underfloor heat pipes.

Quinan, Jack, *Frank Lloyd Wright's Larkin Building, Myth and Fact*, The Architectural History Foundation, New York & MIT Press, Cambridge 1987.

The best book about a single building. It makes the loss even more painful and finally clears up the question about Wright's use of air conditioning. It shows the construction and demolition. One longs for a colour photo, though.

Restoration Committee of the Frank Lloyd Wright Home and Studio Foundation, *The Plan for Restoration and Adaptive Use of The Frank Lloyd Wright Home and Studio*, The University of Chicago Press, Chicago 1977, 1978.

An impressive set of drawings and photographs quantifying a complex building, this book records its many lives under the hand of Wright searching for new ways and means.

Spencer, Robert C, *The Work of Frank Lloyd Wright*, The Architectural Review, Boston, June 1900. Reprinted by the Prairie School Press (Wilbert R Hasbrouck).

Reportedly laid out by Wright, the issue contains much information that is reported nowhere else. The fold-out pages show Wright's graphic drafting abilities. There are also several window designs that we know nothing about.

Wright, Frank Lloyd, *Complete Works*, ADA Edita, Tokyo, 12 Volumes.

A series that publishes most of Wright's drawings other than working drawings. One only wishes that they were a bit larger to show more detail.

OPPOSITE PAGE: Taliesin, Spring Green, Wisconsinl. One of the most beautiful places on earth, this is a near perfect melding of building and nature.